Korean Handicrafts

Art in Everyday Life

KOREA ESSENTIALS No. 20

Korean Handicrafts: Art in Everyday Life

Copyright © 2014 by The Korea Foundation

Published in 2014 by Seoul Selection
B1 Korean Publishers Association Bldg., 6, Samcheong-ro, Jongno-gu, Seoul 03062, Korea
Phone: (82-2) 734-9564
Fax: (82-2) 734-9563
Email: hankinseoul@gmail.com
Website: www.seoulselection.com

ISBN: 978-89-97639-54-0 04080
ISBN: 978-89-91913-70-7 (set)
Printed in the Republic of Korea

Korean Handicrafts

Art in Everyday Life

KOREA FOUNDATION
한국국제교류재단

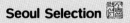

Seoul Selection

CONTENTS

INTRODUCTION

Milan Design Week is perhaps the world's single biggest event in global design, visited by over 300,000 people from 160 countries each year. For the 2013 and 2014 events, something a bit different was on offer: a two-year special exhibition titled *Constancy & Change in Korean Traditional Craft*. Design professionals and media in Italy and all of Europe were impressed and excited by the work on display—pottery, metalwork, textiles, lacquering, and furniture created by a few dozen of the top artisans working in Korean traditional handicrafts today. They praised the artisanal spirit, the way Korean handicrafts makers continue creating beautiful work with traditional values in a digital age dominated by cutting-edge technology.

Since time immemorial, Korea has developed an outstanding craft culture. Its superior quality can be seen in everything from the beautiful and elaborate golden crowns of the Three Kingdoms era (57 BC–AD 668) to the astonishing scientific technology of the Unified Silla era's Seokguram Grotto. Even China, the birthplace of celadon, was bewitched by the magical jade greens found in the celadon of Goryeo. Simple yet sophisticated handicrafts handed down from the Joseon era continue to enjoy great popularity today among Koreans and people around the world. Exquisitely embroidered silks, woven sedge mats and baskets, mother-of-pearl inlay furniture, knots and paper—Korea's crafts truly cast a spell with their multifaceted beauty.

Over the years, these traditional handicrafts were produced to meet human needs. Their artistry reflects centuries of knowledge and technique, honed by a multitude of practitioners. They are practical items for daily life, and their creators have sought to honor their functional role while capturing the fullest of sophisticated beauty. They are true examples of art in life, vessels that capture both the daily experience of their users and the aesthetic values of their time.

This book was written as an introduction to Korean handicrafts and the manner in which they have captured Korea's unique culture and way of life over the millennia. Its chapters examine the characteristics of these works as well as their history—a sample of representative pieces handed down from the past, along with the lives of the people who make them. Finally, it looks at how these traditions have transformed over time and are situated in the present day.

"The art of the craftsman is a bond between the peoples
of the world."

- Florence Dibell Bartlett

1

Chapter One

THE QUALITIES OF KOREAN CRAFTS

The term "craft" refers to an activity where specific skills are used to make everyday items by hand. Creating clothing and fabrics, producing dinnerware and utensils, making the decorations that adorn furniture and homes—all of these are examples of craft. But craft is also about harnessing beauty in the most practical of objects, the things we use in our daily lives. For this reason, some have called it the "nearest of arts" in life. Craft is a vessel that captures the life of its users and the aesthetics of their time.

Beyond the characteristics mentioned above, craft is also an art form that expresses national identity. Craft items are produced in the far reaches of the planet—coast to coast, shoreline to mountaintop—and the materials used for them are as diverse as this broad geography would suggest. Their shapes differ from one use to the next; different castes of users mean different "classes" of craft.

Expressive techniques and production methods also differ between eras and regions. Every foreign form that is introduced goes through a process of adoption and incorporation. Over many years, Koreans have unconsciously developed a character that sets them apart, a cultivated quality that is uniquely their own.

NATURALISM

Like many populations around the world, Koreans have always had a particular reverence for nature, an influence that is felt in many ways. The peninsula's natural environment has provided Koreans

Traditional handicrafts are handmade items featured prominently in Korean daily living, and are steeped in cultural significance in the lives of Korean people.

The extraordinary attachment Koreans have to nature can be seen through Korean traditional handicrafts.

with a set direction for their art, a design aesthetic that, rooted in the worldviews of Daoism and Buddhism, adopts nature as its matrix and the search for beauty in nature as its ideal. The spirit of Korean beauty is a rejection of the artificial. This search for the aesthetic of simplicity bears the influences of Laozi's wu wei (nonaction) and *ziran* (naturalness), and the Buddhist notion of *yathabutham*: seeing things as they really are.

The Korean concept of nature is not that of something to master, but something to adapt to; it is this view that informs the naturalist aesthetic—an emphasis on harmony and balance with nature. The handicrafts produced under this cultural influence have a simple appeal that allows them to harmonize naturally with whatever natural environment in which they are placed. Factor in the

characteristic topography of the Korean Peninsula, with its beauteous lines and colors, and the result is craftwork that is refined in form and elegant in hue.

Naturalism is a fundamental characteristic found in Korean sculptures and earthenware dating back to ancient times. In contrast with the perfectionism and stark expressionism of the Chinese aesthetic, Korean works tend to value the overall impression in lieu of the details, human mildness instead of splendor or detachment, natural contemplation over abstraction. The ancient Korean crafts that survive today are not ritual items such as those of Bronze Age China. Most are connected to daily life, projecting none of the Chinese items' sense of imposing dignity or excessive technique.

Korean craftspeople try to produce works that exist in harmony with nature.

ELEGANCE AND THE ARTISTIC SPIRIT

Most examples of the Korean aesthetic that survive today are craft items from the Joseon era (1392–1910), a time when people sought practical function in the natural spirit. Joseon crafts found their most distinctive characteristic in the daily essentials and writing implements of the aristocratic *yangban* class. Joseon culture was rooted in Confucian philosophy, and the materials used for its crafts were often inexpensive—wood, bamboo, earth, and sedge—all of them in line with the *yangban*'s simple tastes. The unique charm and beauty of this crafting tradition has been carried on to this day, making Joseon crafts some of the most coveted not only by Koreans but by many people around the world.

Admirers have often praised Korean crafts for their directness, their simplicity, and their purity. They have none of the prestige or grandeur one senses with Chinese crafts, none of the affectation or technicality associated with Japanese work. "Technique without technique" is how some have described it, or "design without design."

2

Chapter Two

A HISTORY OF KOREAN CRAFTS

If the origins of crafts lie in people using readily available materials to make the various things they needed to subsist, then it can be argued that they have been with us since the dawn of humankind.

The category of "craft" is quite broad, encompassing household items, furniture, and other accessories that people have devised to make their lives more comfortable and convenient. Even a look at the different materials shows an astonishing level of diversity: metal, stone, wood, lacquer, bamboo, paper, leather, fired clay, wax, and glass, to name just a sample. There are the religious items used at temples and lectures, each specialized for different classes and uses. There are royal items, epitomizing contemporary technology and art with their expression of the ruler's majesty and prestige. Then there are the household items—ornamental and ornate expressions of the economic abundance and power of aristocratic society, or pure reflections of the working classes, called "folk art" for the way they represent the lives of the masses.

Each era in Korean history bears its own unique developments. We find exquisite mirrors from the Neolithic Era, echoing the modern aesthetic with their ornamental patterns in geometric lines. Finely detailed bronze mirrors; crowns and earrings from the Goguryeo, Baekje, Silla, and Gaya periods, all exhibiting an artful mastering of all manner of gold and silver techniques originating in distant Central Asia; Goryeo celadon, renowned in world pottery history for its artistry; the simple white porcelain and *buncheong* ware, concise yet refreshing wooden furnishings, and splendid yet dignified mother-of-pearl lacquerware of the Joseon period—all are expressions of the ideas, techniques, and artistry of their time.

The chief materials for Korean crafts are metal, wood, and clay. The following sections give a brief introduction to their development over the years.

Ancient Korean earthenware

METAL CRAFTS

It was in the Bronze Age—sometime around 700 BC—that metal crafts first appeared in Korea. The first items produced in bronze were objects used in religious ceremonies, weapons of war, and accessories for horse carts. Sophisticated in their technology, their quality was on par with items produced by other cultures in other regions around the same time.

Metalwork became even more elaborate by the fourth and fifth centuries, a quality seen in many surviving gold relics unearthed from ancient tombs. The period including both the Three Kingdoms and the Unified Silla era marked the peak for the variety of tools

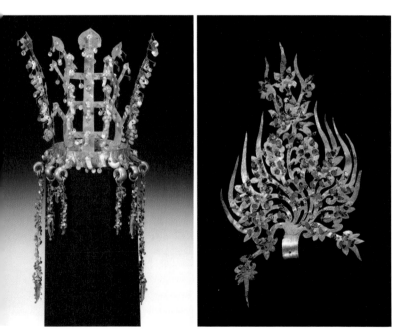

Left: A gold crown excavated from the north mound of a Silla tomb in Hwangnam, Gyeongju
Right: An elaborate gold ornament that was attached to the silk burial cap of King Muryeong (r. 501–523) of Baekje

Elaborate gold earrings decorated with gold threads from the Bubuchong Tomb near Gyeongju

produced and metals used. Metalwork managed to hang on through the Goryeo period (918–1392) before quickly fading away in the Joseon era (1392–1910).

The work produced since the Three Kingdoms period can be classified into four categories: ornaments; Buddhist paraphernalia and *sarira*, or Buddhist relics; and daily items. Some of the ornaments that have been found include gold and gilt bronze headpieces, along with necklaces, earrings, bracelets, belts, and waistbands constructed in precious metals such as gold and silver. Astonishing strides in form and technique took place during the Three Kingdoms period, but the production of such

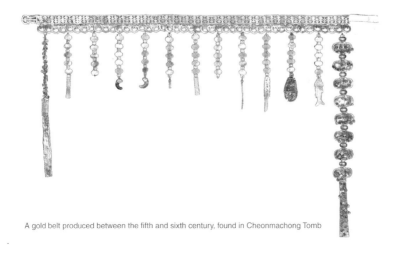

A gold belt produced between the fifth and sixth century, found in Cheonmachong Tomb

Beautiful Baekje incense burner

Buddhist bell from Sudeoksa Temple in Yesan-gun, Chungcheongnam-do

items entered a steep decline during the Unified Silla period (676–935).

The realm of Buddhist paraphernalia consists of items used by monks in Buddhist events and temples. Perhaps the most noteworthy are the incense burners, two varieties of bells (bronze and gold, with different shapes), and *kundika*, or water vessels. The number of Buddhism-related relics increased as the era of Unified Silla moved forward, and significant advances were made in bronze mirrors, *beomjong* (temple bells), and incense burners in the subsequent Goryeo period.

While some of the items discovered in old tombs and stone

pagodas were made from metal or silver, most were cast in bronze. An especially large number of bronze mirrors from the Goryeo period have been found. Although there have been similar items from other periods as well, no other era matches them for their variety of shapes and patterns.

More exquisite technique can be found in the forms and patterns of the burial accessories excavated from Three Kingdoms tombs, or the delicate metal inlay patterns created with the metalwork of Goryeo.

WOODWORK

Wood is a fragile material, and most wooden relics that still remain intact were produced relatively late in their corresponding periods in history. There are some wooden items that have been found in Three Kingdoms tombs, but most are so badly decayed that it is impossible to determine their original appearance; rare, indeed, is the item that is wholly preserved. Most of the surviving examples are lacquered, and in some cases, only the lacquer remains.

Besides varnishing, another technique used with wood was *najeon* (mother-of-pearl inlay), a form of decoration in which iridescent pieces of shell in various shapes were embedded or otherwise applied. Mother-of-pearl techniques became very advanced in the Goryeo period; their reputation became so widely known that the Song Dynasty

Furniture with mother-of-pearl inlay

envoy Xu Jing praised their exquisiteness in his *Gaoli Tujing* (Illustrated Account of Goryeo). When a queen of Yuan ordered mother-of-pearl scripture cases, she turned to Goryeo's craftspeople to deliver pieces of adequate quality.

In addition to the mother-of-pearl work, many wood items from the Joseon era are prime examples of traditional carpentry. One of the key characteristics of wood furnishings from this period is that they were designed to suit the living environment. Techniques emphasized the wood's type and grain, highlighting the pattern in a way that infused the item with nature. In this sense, these pieces are

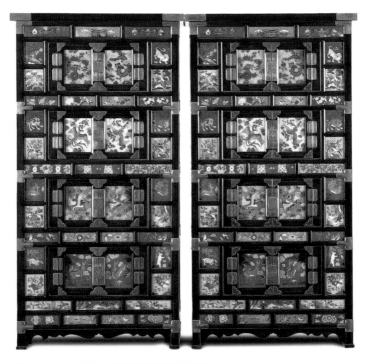

Four-tier chests with *hwagak* (painted oxhorn) decoration

Mother-of-pearl inlay handicrafts

perhaps the best expression of the reverence for nature in Korean art.

Hwagak, or hornwork, is another form of Joseon-era woodwork that has drawn attention for its intricate detail. *Hwagak* items were produced by soaking the horns of young bulls in warm water and spreading them out into thin, transparent layers, which were then decorated with folk art images using white, blue, red, green, yellow, and black pigment and attached to wood. These were often women's items, ranging in size from fine-toothed combs to four-tier chests. Bamboo items were also common. A particularly elegant example is *nakjuk*, where patterns were seared onto the pale surface of bamboo wood using hot irons.

The Joseon-era *sarangbang* (gentleman's parlor) was typically decorated with materials and items that would evoke a sense of simplicity—austerity, almost. It was in the *anbang* (the women's room) that more splendid items featuring mother-of-pearl, *hwagak*, and the like were displayed. Kitchen furnishings tended toward the practical and solid.

During this time, it was common practice to varnish the surfaces of wooden furniture with either unboiled lacquer, yellowish-red lacquer, or black lacquer. During the Silla era, the government established a position known as *chiljeon* (lacquer craftsman), and high-quality, unboiled lacquer remained in continued use until the Joseon period. Surfaces were also decorated with functional features—locks, hinges, and handles of iron, tin, and nickel—as well as structural features such as splice plates, studs, and trimmings.

POTTERY

When humans began producing containers and utensils, the first material they turned to was the earth beneath their feet. Earthenware has become something of a catchall term for the different pieces that ancient societies made with earth, but the materials, forms, and surface decorations all became much more diverse as production techniques developed over the years.

The earthenware items of the Three Kingdoms era, for

Comb-pattern pottery used in the Korean Peninsula during the Neolithic period

Horse rider—shaped earthenware vessels excavated from Geumnyeongchong Tomb in Gyeongju

example, are quite clearly distinct, each representing a combination of distinct cultural traits. Some of the earthenware from Goguryeo is cylindrical in shape and features three short legs. These are a stark contrast to the white, almost gray urns of Baekje and the *gobae*, or mounted cups, and long-necked bottles of Silla. Some of the most outstanding examples include the horseman earthenware and boat-shaped pottery of Gyeongju's Geumnyeongchong tombs.

Around the 10th century, the general desire for earthenware vessels began to lessen in favor of porcelain ones. It was a time of great change in materials, shapes, patterns, and glazes—the dawn of the celadon era. First developed in China, Goryeo celadon techniques were refined in the late 10th century before reaching their zenith in the early 1100s.

The porcelains of Goryeo marked a break from the more exultant styles of old. Notably, they transformed into practical items, specialized for their function, and went on to become increasingly diverse in type, surface pattern, and expressive style.

Celadon can be divided into several categories. In addition to pure celadon, with no other shades than blue, other varieties include inlaid, cinnabar, chrysanthemum, and marble ware. Inlaid celadon work involved the same techniques applied with mother-of-pearl in woodwork and metal inlays in metalwork and was very unique in the pottery world when it was first devised by the potters of Goryeo.

The late Goryeo period saw the introduction of oxidized flame firing techniques from the Chinese Yuan Dynasty. Stamping methods were also introduced, a practice carried on into the *buncheong* work of the Joseon era. That period would bring major changes in shapes, coloring, patterns,

Celadon Fish Dragon-Shaped Ewer
(Goryeo Dynasty)

Korean Melon-Shaped Celadon Bottle with Peony
and Chrysanthemum Flowers (Goryeo Dynasty)

Incense Burner, Celadon
with Openwork Design
(Goryeo Dynasty)

and inlay technique. Gone was the small-mouthed, top-heavy design of the prunus vase (*maebyeong*), considered the representative form of the Goryeo era. In its place were long-necked vases and tools for writing (inkwells, containers for making ink), produced in mass quantities. White became the dominant color; Confucian motifs were chosen for patterns.

The wares of this new era, a style called *buncheong*, were humbler, simpler, and less rigid in design. This approach also influenced the types of patterns used, with designs that tended toward a less-structured composition rather than a symmetrical or otherwise rigidly designed one. *Buncheong* techniques were quite fashionable for a time, but their popularity also began to decline. By the beginning of the Japanese Invasions of the late 16th century, they were gone

Maebyeong, Buncheong (Goryeo Dynasty)

Jar, White Porcelain with Plum, Bamboo, and Bird
Design in Underglaze Cobalt Blue (Joseon Dynasty)

Roof and eaves tiles

entirely.

The dawn of the Joseon era saw the introduction of a new style of pottery, though there was overlap between this and the *buncheong* works. Introduced in the early days and continuing through to the dynasty's end in 1910, white porcelain eventually became the dominant form of pottery, with cobalt blue designs over a pale base being especially common. Originally called *hoecheong* or *hoehoecheong* (Mohammedan blue) the dyes used in this style were first brought into Korea—and China—by Arabian merchants from Persia. The designs applied to porcelain were heavily Confucian in character, most of them representing the riches of the secular world or literary and poetic sensibilities. Brushwork was adopted as a technique, with design-based expression giving way to a more painterly approach.

Another important area of pottery was tile and brick. Tiles were made by kneading earth, pressing it into a frame, and firing it for use on rooftops. Other tiles were attached to eaves; called *wadang*, they were capped with end pieces and carved with ornamental patterns. Many changes in form and pattern can be observed in tiles over the period from the Three Kingdoms to the Joseon era. Lotus flowers were a dominant motif, while additional decorations included other plants, animals, demons (used to ward off evil), and Buddhist designs.

MODERN KOREAN HANDICRAFT

In 1876, the Joseon government signed the Treaty of Amity with Japan on Ganghwado Island. Six years later came the US–Korea Treaty of Peace, Amity, Commerce, and Navigation of 1882. This period marked the true arrival of modern Western civilization into the country, which had theretofore adopted a policy of strict isolation, and much conflict would ensue. Japanese and Chinese merchants began introducing Westernized daily essentials through the ports of Incheon and Busan. The blow to traditional craftspeople—Joseon's producers of textiles, paper, and brassware—was immediate.

The next 35 years would witness the decline of the Joseon Dynasty and the signing of the Japan–Korea Annexation Treaty of 1910. It was a period of existential crisis for Korean culture, as all the lifestyle patterns of Japan (which had recently undergone its own successful modernization) began percolating into society. For the traditional craft makers and artisans of Joseon, it meant a full-scale collapse. Specialists in mother-of-pearl lacquerware, pottery, and woodwork did manage to thrive somewhat, their survival

A master bowyer imparting his craft to his son

owing in many ways to the Japanese taste for antiques. Japanese scholars like Yanagi Muneyoshi voiced their fondness and respect for the aesthetic world created by the Koreans, and efforts were made to discover the Korean people's craft culture and develop the traditions of the craft arts.

After liberation from Japanese rule in 1945 and the experience of the Korean War (1950–1953), the country lay in ruin and chaos, yet even then the rebuilding and reestablishment of Korean craft traditions was made a priority. The year 1946 saw the creation of the Korea Craft Association, with the goal of broadening the base for qualitative improvements in crafts. This was followed in 1949 by the founding of the National Art Exhibition. Design education was revived as craft departments were instituted at Seoul National University, Hongik University, and Ewha Womans University. Premodern concepts were abandoned, and crafts became a field of design on par with other fine arts.

The period around 1970 brought even greater variety to craft activities, as forums for the art broadened from government exhibitions to private, group, and solo showings, along with the

People appreciating the highest award winner at the 1975 National Art Exhibition

National Art Exhibition. Opportunities for university-level craft education increased dramatically, and the graduates from these departments became a base for potential development of the field. But while the number of higher education institutions and art competitions was proliferating, their focus was mainly on luxury items, and the crafts themselves began drifting away from their original social role as everyday items. It was in the 2000s that crafts gained renewed recognition as an area of cultural production, and the focus of education shifted once again to practical items for the general public.

A SELECTION OF KOREAN CRAFTS

GOLD LEAF DECORATION

Gold leaf typically refers to a form of gold that has been pounded down to very thin sheets. In Korea, it has also come to describe the technique of using adhesives to attach gold leaf designs to objects. The earliest record of gold leaf use dates back to Egypt's Fourth Dynasty (c. 2613–2494 BC), the golden age of this ancient civilization. According to the *Samguk sagi* (History of the Three Kingdoms), an ancient Korean text published in 1145, a system was in place under Korea's King Heungdeok of Unified Silla (r. 826–836) that indicated differing status with gold leaf patterns applied to clothing.

  People often think of gold leaf work as a simple process of applying patterns on fabric, but the traditional process was a series of quite complex and demanding steps. During the Joseon era, palaces employed different technicians for each one: one craftsman to refine the gold, another to hammer it flat, still another to carve the patterns into wood, a fourth to make the glue, and a fifth to apply the gold leaf to the fabric.

Important Components: Plates and Glue

The Unified Silla and Goryeo eras saw a flowering of Buddhist culture in Korea. Gold and silver pigments were used to decorate paintings of the Buddha, and monks dressed in clothes with gold leaf patterns. The use of beauteous gold leaf patterns in Korea's temples would fade away during the Joseon era, which suppressed Buddhism in favor of Confucianism. Now the designs were only permitted in the royal house. Even there, gold leaf was not used on ordinary dress. There was also a strict, hierarchal order to the

Clothing with *geumbak* (gold leaf) print patterns

patterns used: flowers alone for the princess, flower and phoenix designs for the queen. Outfits for the queen mother included the flower, the phoenix, and the dragon. Gold leaf plating was applied in designs to show the wearer's noble status: Letters, flowers, fruit, birds, insects, other animals, and geometric patterns were used.

The gold leaf process involves a series of separate stages. There is

Joseon Dynasty queen dress with *geumbak*-printed patterns

During the Joseon Dynasty, *geumbak*-printed attire was reserved solely for the royal family, but since the first half of the 20th century, it has been adopted by commoners for auspicious events such as weddings.

the drawing of the pattern, usually on paper. Next comes the production of the plate by transferring the pattern to wood. The glue must be produced and applied to the plate, the location for applying the plate to fabric must be marked, and the plate must be applied before the glue on the fabric has fully dried. After this come the drying and the touching up. These steps may sound simple, but each one requires the skill of a veteran craft maker, along with a deep understanding of the properties of the fabric, gold, and glue.

One of the more crucial aspects of each plate's construction is that the design on its surface must be engraved perfectly. Next is the matter of the glue. Glues differ in consistency, depending on the thickness and dye of the fabric. The weather on the date of application must also be taken into account when choosing the right consistency.

Over the course of the 20th century, as the Joseon Dynasty ended and the Japanese occupation took hold, gold-leafed clothing spread

around the country. It was adopted first by Korean noble families, and then by ordinary ones, for special occasions such as weddings and 60th birthdays (an occasion for particular celebration in Korea). Even today, you will find people who don gold leaf designs for major events.

Gold leaf master Kim Deok-hwan

RAMIE FABRIC

Alongside *sambe* (hemp clothing), ramie garments can be considered among Korea's most representative traditional summer attire. *Sambe* is a coarse-textured fabric woven from the fibers of a type of cannabis plant and was once used to make the everyday clothing of common people. In contrast, ramie is a delicate fabric painstakingly woven from ramie plant fibers. Befitting the arduous weaving process, ramie garments became associated with the elite sections of Korean society and were presented as tributes to kings of the Joseon Dynasty. This fabric is so exquisitely thin, admirers would compare its lightness to dragonfly wings.

Many places in the Jeolla-do produce ramie, but the Hansan region of Seocheon-gun, Chungcheongnam-do has long been known for its high-quality ramie. Yi Jung-hwan (1690–1756), a Joseon Dynasty scholar of the School of Practical Learning (Silhak), wrote of various regional specialties in the distinguished geography book

1. Hansan ramie
2. Fashion models exhibiting collections made of Hansan ramie
3. Traditional *hanbok* made with Hansan ramie

RAMIE WEAVING PROCESS

When weaving ramie, the warp threads are first adjusted to be vertical and the woof is set up in the cross direction. The woof threads are then wound around a traditional *buk* (spool) for the weaving to begin. The warp beam is laid down on the loom and threads are pulled out of the reed for the two to be alternately woven. The reed is rethreaded and the thread tightened with a loom roller. Using the foot to depress the treadle allows the rotating horizontal bar for warp threads to be lifted up enough to allow the *buk* to be passed through. One *pil* of ramie fabric can be completed in four to five days using this weaving process.

Taengniji (Ecological Guide to Korea), which included tobacco from Jinan, ginger from Jeonju, sedge from Andong and Yean, and ramie from Imcheon and Hansan. It was said that every household in Hansan grew ramie in their fields and that all Hansan womenfolk wove ramie fabric. Hansan ramie is revered for its superior quality, so fine yet durable that "Hansan fine ramie" has become a proper noun in its own right, with the phrase suggesting that one *pil* (bolt) of the fabric could fit into a rice bowl.

QUILTING

The term *nubi* refers to quilted clothing made by placing a cotton lining between two pieces of fabric and then sewing the three pieces together with close stitching. This lining provides a layer of insulation, making these clothes ideal for protection against the cold. Quilting was once used to make everyday garments, protective armor for soldiers, clothing for monks, and bedding items. With the advent of the modern sewing machine, traditional quilting, once an integral aspect of everyday life in Korea, is slowly disappearing. Remnants of traditional quilting now remain due to the steadfast resolution of artisans who self-study this traditional craft.

Children's *hanbok* made with quilting

Historical Background and Uses of Quilting

While cotton is the usual quilt-lining material, it is said that other plant material, animal fur, and leather have been used on occasion in lieu of cotton. The first known quilting artifact is a typical cotton-lined quilted garment recovered in April 1974 from a Joseon-period tomb of the Gwangju Lee clan. Later on, in June 1981, 16 pieces of double-layered quilted clothing of a non-cotton material were excavated from a Joseon-period tomb of Prince Tamneunggun (1636–1731), a member of the Lee clan of Jeonju.

Quilted clothing is largely divided into cold-weather wear, protective armor, and religious attire. Due to its lining layer, quilted clothing is excellent at retaining warmth even when compared to other fabric of similar thickness. The late Joseon Dynasty period genre painter Sin Yun-bok often depicted scholars and courtesans in quilted clothing in his works. In Joseon Dynasty documents that recorded the type and quantity of items used at court events, several kinds of quilting were mentioned: *omongnubi* (inset stitching),

napjangnubi (surface stitching), and *jannubi* (fine stitching).

A notable example of quilted protective wear can be seen in a wall mural found inside Gamsinchong, a Goguryeo-era tomb, which included a figure wearing armor. The crisscrossing design of the attire's diagonal and horizontal lines suggest that it was a quilted piece. Over the years, a number of quilted artifacts serving dual purposes have been uncovered, including armor and helmets made with cotton or paper lining to enhance both combat and thermal protection. In terms of religious attire, quilted robes have historically been worn by Buddhist monks, with their patchwork garments often appearing weatherworn due to regular wear. One hypothesis regarding the historical evolution of quilted garments is that they were adopted by Buddhist monks first before eventually being embraced by the common people, a transition that resulted from the general practicality and durability of such a wardrobe.

Distinctive Features of Quilted Clothing

Not only does hand-stitched quilting boast better thermal and air circulation properties than machine-sewn garments, quilting is strong and threads do not unravel easily. More than anything else, to Koreans, a quilted garment is much more than something to be worn; it represents the maker's heartfelt sentiments. In the past, people put extreme care and effort into quilting, such that these garments took on a meaning of affection and were presented as gifts on special occasions: for the elderly on their 60th birthday, newborn babies, young men sitting the civil service examination, and soldiers going off to war. Even though quilting is found in various cultures around the world, Korean quilting can be argued to differ from other varieties because, rather than focus on partial quilting, a technique practiced in many quilting cultures around the world, Korean quilting is applied in a uniform way over the entire surface, with emphasis placed on meticulous craftsmanship.

SHOE MAKING

Korea's traditional *hanbok* clothing has sometimes been called the "clothing of the wind." It's a term to describe the natural beauty of the curved lines, like traces left by a passing breeze. By this logic, traditional Korean shoes, known as *hwa* (shoes that extend above the ankle) and *hye* (shoes that stop below the ankle), could fairly be called "shoes of the wind." The sleek lines connecting the top of the *hye* to its heel recall the "fish belly line" of the *hanbok* jacket (*jeogori*), while the swelling tip echoes the elegance of the shapely *beoseon* sock.

A *hwahyejang* is a shoemaker who specializes in traditional Korea shoes, derived from the Joseon-era catchall term to address all makers of *hwa* and *hye*. These two types of shoes date back to ancient times and were worn according to one's occupation: The horse-riding cultures of the north appear to have typically worn

leather boots (*hwa*), while the farmers of the south wore shoes of leather or straw (*hye*).

Over time, Korea's traditional shoes went beyond mere functionality and became markers of status—as well as things of beauty. Decoration was a painstaking process, with records of *hwa* boots bedecked in gold and silk from the Goguryeo period. Goryeo craft makers were especially renowned for their technique, with the kingdom maintaining a system to manage the most

Traditional Korean footwear *hye* (shoes without necks) and *hwa* (shoes with necks)

highly skilled of them. By the time the Joseon era had started, the central government offices boasted 16 makers of *hwa* and 14 makers of *hye*.

A 72-Step Process

More than 20 kinds of shoes are said to have existed in Joseon-era Korea. They differed by a future wearer's gender and status, as well as the time and place in which they would be worn. The king and queen wore a special type known as a *seok*, while civil and military officials wore high boots with their uniforms. Boots were made of deerskin, sheepskin, and silk; a waterproof *suhwaja* style was also worn. *Hye* were worn chiefly by the upper class, with a low rim covering the top surface. Men and women wore different types, with noblemen of the middle Joseon period adopting the *taesahye* style to symbolize an era of peace. (Before that, they had often worn

Female footwear, *danghye*

the more feminine *danghye* variety.) *Taesahye* had relatively shallow rims and were girded in unpatterned silk or sheepskin. The upper toe was broad and high, while the point and heel were decorated with an arabesque pattern known as the *taesamun*.

The *danghye* was a woman's shoe that featured an equally lovely arabesque design. Women also favored the *unhye*, or "cloud shoe," which had a bamboo flower design on the tip. Its sleek shape earned it the name *jebiburi sin*, or "swallow's beak shoe." The *heukpihye* was made with black leather, while the oil-treated *yuhye* was worn on rainy days. The *onhye*, or "warm shoe," was covered with cotton flannel or other warm fabrics that helped promote heat retention. Commoners often wore straw shoes or hemp-cord sandals.

A defining characteristic of the *hye* is its curvilinear beauty, a slim, sleek arch from the relatively low toes to the heel. This clean, unruffled shape can be attributed to the firm leather and cloth lining used to make the shoe. For the lining, a mixture of cotton and ramie or hemp was covered in layers of rice starch and left to dry in the natural winds, sunlight, and dew for about three days. This process of repeated moistening and drying is what gave the lining its characteristic stiffness. The shoe pattern was then applied to the lining and cut out. Next came the side material, applied to the area above and below the rim like bias tape. After that, an extra layer of cloth was placed over top to serve as a kind of pillar, bearing the weight on the rim and securing the shape. The inner skin was then cut out and carefully applied with rice paste inside the rim, where the cloth lining was placed. Needles for threading the toe, heel, rim, and sole were fashioned out of hairs from the neck of a mountain boar.

MOTHER-OF-PEARL INLAY

Some things only deepen in their beauty with time—things like wardrobes and dressers passed down over the years, stationery chests, and dressing tables. Perhaps the best example of beauty maturing over the years can be found with mother-of-pearl lacquerware: lacquered pieces finished with embedded or attached patterns of abalone and conch shell. In Korea, works of mother-of-

pearl inlay were often found in the furniture and accessories of the *anbang* or the *seojae* (the study where men read books). They added dignity to the setting, while also hinting at the prestige of the owner. Passed down as heirlooms, they provided a glimpse at the family background.

Still Beautiful after a Thousand Years

Two different words are used in Korean to refer to mother-of-pearl: the more general *najeon*, as well as *jagae*. *Jagae* is a term for lacquered ornaments finished with mother-of-pearl, though in its strict sense it refers specifically to abalone or conch shells sliced down to a fine thickness. The techniques of paring the mother-of-pearl down and attaching it can be separated into two types: cutting (*kkeuneumjil*), where long, threadlike slices of mother-of-pearl are cut along straight or diagonal lines, and filing (*jureumjil*), in which a jigsaw is used for carving out the overall pattern.

Both the mother-of-pearl and the lacquer are key parts of these pieces. The best mother-of-pearl in Korea is believed to come from

the South Sea and Jejudo Island, which is also the reason Tongyeong mother-of-pearl inlay work developed in the way that it did. In contrast, the best lacquer is said to come from Wonju in Gangwon-do. There are over 80 known species of lacquer tree around the world, but Wonju's variety stands out for its durability and germ-killing properties.

Perhaps it is the way that lacquered items resist change over the centuries, or their characteristic beauty, but varnishing is a nearly universal practice the whole world over. Vietnam is especially well-known for its lacquers, while

Myanmar has earned renown for lacquer painting. But when it comes to lacquer crafts, the three countries of Korea, China, and Japan stand head and shoulders above the rest. Common wisdom has it that mother-of-pearl lacquerware was introduced to Korea from China's Tang Dynasty during the Three Kingdoms period. But as China went on to develop the *diaoqi* technique of varnishing delicate sculpted patterns on its items, Korea blazed its own trail with mother-of-pearl work. Japan, which acquired its lacquer

Painting lacquerware

techniques through Korea, would also go on to focus more on pictorial methods using lacquer powder rather than mother-of-pearl.

Making mother-of-pearl lacquerware is a long process of repetition and patience. It takes no fewer than 45 stages—spanning more than six months—before an item is finished. The very first step is to apply unboiled lacquer to the wooden base (also called the skeleton). Unboiled lacquer (*saeng-ot* in Korean) is a transparent, clear syrup made of boiled down lacquer tree sap. This first step is taken to avoid warping of the wood. Hemp cloth or ramie is applied over top, also to prevent warping (since the item is to be used for centuries, if not millennia), and to better enable the object to absorb the lacquer. A mixture of lacquer with rice starch and charcoal powder is then applied over the cloth, the latter providing damp-proofing and moth-proofing properties. Then a mixture of red clay and lacquer is added over top. Next, the surface is polished evenly with a whetstone, washed clean, and then varnished again. Only after this process is complete can the mother-of-pearl be applied. Once the object is polished smooth, it is now time to apply the opal-like coloring of the mother-of-pearl.

The filing process used to create the mother-of-pearl pattern requires the most delicate of techniques and an artist's touch. The steps themselves are not difficult, but sketching and excising the pattern are quite demanding tasks. Even the slightest trembling or hesitation is enough to ruin the tracing of arabesque or chrysanthemum patterns with a fine brush.

Forging a new tradition

Once the mother-of-pearl is applied, the lacquering process begins again: repeated steps of priming, coating, and painting over, then polishing and beginning again. It is here that we find the key to the mystery of lacquer—what allows it to resist fading or decay over thousands of years, as in the tomb paintings of Goguryeo or the Heavenly Horse painting from the Silla period. After the final coat

is applied, the lacquer is scraped away, each delicate touch of the craft maker revealing more and more of the mother-of-pearl's brilliant coloration.

The best mother-of-pearl comes from abalone, but it is often used together with conch shell or pearl oyster to add powerful points for greater artistry. Each type

Lacquering techniques as seen in modern furniture

adds a different color, injecting a sense of perspective in the two-dimensional pattern. Some of the most common motifs are the ten symbols of longevity, so named because they represent long life without death; these include the sun, the mountain, the pine tree, the moon, the cloud, the elixir plant, and the crane. Other designs include arabesques, birds, and flowers such as peonies or chrysanthemums.

METAL ORNAMENTS

Confucian beliefs emphasized distinctions between men and women, and their influence over the centuries is felt in the clear divisions of the traditional Korean home into men's and women's spaces. The *sarangbang* was a male space, furnished with concise and humble items—simple like the face of the *seonbi* (Confucian scholar). The women's *anbang*, in contrast, boasted furniture that was more decorative and soft. Wood furniture excelled in its proportion and plainness, and metal ornaments (*duseok*) were the chief elements used to give it its characteristic attitude.

Duseok (also known as *jangseok*) is a metal craft that epitomizes both the beauty and functionality of Korean traditional woodwork in general, and wood furniture in particular. It comes in many types,

Engagement gift box adorned with *duseok* (metal ornaments)

depending on the type of metals and proportions used. There is nickel *jangseok*, its sparkling silver hue recalling fallen snow on a winter tree. Other forms include gold-hued brass, black cast iron, and yellowish tin varieties. Hinged *jangseok* highlight the functionality of sliding components, which move up and down or left to right depending on the purpose. Clasp *jangseok* have three surfaces that come together into a three-dimensional corner that provides a snug embrace. In clamp *jangseok*, two or three surfaces are solidly joined at a right angle or in a "C" shape. Handle *jangseok* are used to open drawers and doors, while lock-base *jangseok* are used to hold up locks.

The metal fittings used on men's furniture emphasized functionality, while those used on women's furniture included elaborate decorations on a functional base. As the Joseon period entered its final days, ornamentation became more of a focus, and the province of Gyeongsang-do—the city of Tongyeong most especially—became a major center for development. Prized among the traditional women's furnishings of Korea, Tongyeong mother-of-pearl lacquerware involved applying a deep black layer of lacquer to furniture, which was then finished with brilliant bits of abalone or conch shell. Metal ornaments were chosen accordingly: brilliant silvery nickel in beautiful designs of butterflies, flowers, cranes, clouds, songbirds, and plum trees.

Alloys: The Artisan's Work

The tin-nickel (*baekdong*) used in ornaments was a seven-to-three mixture of the two elements. These days, the best alloys tend to be factory-made, but the artisans of the past did their own alloy work. The proportions had to be exact: too much tin and the ornament might lose color, too much nickel and it would be too fragile. The melting process for the tin-nickel mixture was said to be as important as the yearly harvest; back in the 1970s and 1980s, artisans assembled for traditional shamanistic ceremonies in which they would pray for the proper mixing of their alloys.

The process of estimating thickness and creating the right nickel plate for the purpose and design involves heating to 1,300 degrees Celsius some 20 to 50 times, with thousands of hammer blows required to flatten out the metal. An engraving knife is used on the outer surface of the plate—made into an even sheet with a thickness of about 0.5 to 1 millimeter, depending on the purpose—to give the characteristic clear silvery sheen.

Duseok of a bat pattern

When using alloys to make plates for engraving, a stencil is applied to the back of the plate and trimmed with a straw cutter, while a chisel is used for three-dimensional effect. After that, a knife is used to carve a pattern on the front. A pattern may be inlaid with dark copper or another metal mixed with gold or silver for an added finish. Once the pattern has been engraved, holes are punched for the nails and the piece is filed down and polished with fabric coated in earthenware powder. The result, simple and unfrivolous, is a tin-nickel ornament with a deep silvery color.

The Meanings of Patterns

Furniture decorated with solid and beautiful metal accents or ornaments can brighten even the dimmest room. An old saying holds that a well-made ornament fits the smallest curve of the wood

Duseok of a butterfly pattern

and is light like a flower petal—yet deceptively strong: The furniture may crumble, but ornament never will. Like the jewelry designer polishing a raw stone, the ornament maker forms different patterns in the surface. And what patterns they are: numbering over 2,000, they include animal motifs like butterflies, bats, and goldfish; flowers like chrysanthemums, daffodils, and lotuses; and many more still in letters and geometric motifs.

Each and every pattern is a reflection of the designer's intent. *Hwajeop* patterns (flowers and butterflies) symbolize marital harmony, while bats represent fecundity and fortune. Goldfish locks can often be found on the furniture used by wives, or the chests where they stored their rice. The saying goes that goldfish ward off disaster because they live in the water and guard fortunes because they sleep with their eyes open. They also lay many eggs, and thus express a wish for fertility, while their small mouths were believed to keep in any riches that entered. For the menfolk's *sarangbang*, furniture decorations often featured a bamboo motif, representing the Confucian ideals of loyalty and filial piety and the dignity and integrity of the noble man.

SOBAN

Doubling as both a tray for carrying food and a dining table, the small *soban* (tray-table) has become an integral part of Korean mealtimes. Historically, it was used in the royal palace to present specialty foods to the king and to carry freshly drawn well water to women's quarters, where one might be praying for a baby. If so blessed, the child would later eat meals from such a table. When there was a death in the household, the *soban* also served as a ritual table for the incense burner to be placed.

Top: *Gujokban* ("dog legs" *soban*)
Bottom: *Hojokban* ("tiger legs" *soban*)

Rooted in Tradition

The *soban* was an essential household item in the traditional Korean home, where people typically sat on *ondol*-heated floors to dine. Food cooked in the kitchen would be carried on these tray-tables to the living quarters, where the meal was eaten off the *soban* while one was seated on the floor. In addition to fulfilling this need, the *soban* was also used for writing purposes and as a tea table.

The earliest evidence of *soban* can be found in wall murals of tombs dating from the Goguryeo Kingdom (37 BC–AD 668). The mural of Gakjeochong (Tomb of the Wrestlers) depicted various items within a home, while the Muyongchong (Tomb of the Dancers) rendering showed a seated government official and Buddhist monk being served food on *soban*.

During the Unified Silla, Goryeo, and Joseon periods, the government retained state-sponsored *soban* craftspeople who were dedicated to the production and supply of the tables. Given that Confucianism called for segregation by gender, age, and social status, it was the custom during the Joseon Dynasty for people to be served and to eat from individual *soban*. For this reason, it was necessary for the table to be compact in size, usually no more than 50 centimeters in length, 30 centimeters in width, and 30 centimeters in height, so that it could be easily handled.

Today's vestiges of the *soban* are largely derived from late Joseon styles, including examples that have been named after their region of origin, such as Haejuban, Tongyeongban, and Najuban. There are also types named for their leg shape, such as *gujokban* ("dog legs") and *hojokban* ("tiger legs"). *Soban* are also categorized by their configuration, including circular, rectangular, and polygonal shapes.

The Reform of 1894 led to Korea's modernization, and with this, a wide availability of tables with folding legs. The introduction of Western furniture too has led to a change in Korean meal-eating, and with more use of dining tables and chairs, *soban* use dropped. Nonetheless, a small number of craftspeople have kept this tradition alive.

Silver Inlay

As a material, metal is cold yet beautiful, simple yet sturdy. It has been valued since ancient times, its surface engraved with rare and beautiful patterns. Metal inlay, a traditional Korean decorative technique, first emerged as part of this process. In metal inlay, thin, threadlike strands of gold, silver, or copper are applied over metal without soldering. The resulting designs, beautiful and delicate, are like embroideries on metal.

Metal inlay represents the very essence of Korean metal crafts. The embroidering of gorgeous patterns on iron or bronze objects with thin, lustrous threads is a process where the artist's touch finds its fullest expression.

Work by Hong Jeong-sil

The Line of Beauty

Examples of metal inlay can be found as far back as Iron Age relics (c. 300 BC–AD 300). The craft was also one of the premier forms of metal work that flourished under the Goryeo and Joseon eras. Korea is obviously not the only country in the world to decorate its metal—many places have used techniques similar to metal inlay. What makes Korea's inlay truly unique is that it is an "art of lines."

Produced through the practice of arranging a series of consistently placed lines, inlay patterns are plain yet artistic, simple yet playful. The images reflect the hopes of people in the time they were made: riches and honor, long life, fecundity, and abundance. The ten aforementioned symbols of longevity seen in *najeonjang* can be found in *ipsajang* works as well: designs of flowers and birds, grasses and insects, or natural landscapes, such as a duck strolling along a stream with dropping willows overhead. Everyday items such as candlesticks, braziers, cigarette cases, locks, and stationery were some of pieces decorated with the technique; the use of inlay on such common objects was a way of keeping fine and traditional things close at all times, helping the owner keep composed and enjoy some moments of leisure.

Another defining feature of Korea's inlay is the heavy use of silver. This was partly due to the scarcity of gold in the region, but the real reason may more accurately be associated with national identity. In the words of Japanese folk art researchers and art critic Yanagi Muneyoshi, silver is "a beauty that hides its light within." More specifically, silver is somewhat plain when presented on its own, but when combined with other metals, it complements their beauty with a distinct charm—delicate yet lasting. It is perhaps this quality that has made it resonate so strongly with Korean emotions and explains why silver is the dominant metal for inlay work. Also known as "silver stamping" or "silver threading," *ipsajang* has become the Korean metal craft par excellence.

Two techniques have chiefly been used for inlay work: *kkium* (insertion) and *jjoeum* (chiseling). Widely used in the Goryeo period, insertion involved carving out a pattern in metal with a chisel and placing the silver threading inside. Because of the country's reverence for Buddhism at the time, most of these pieces were examples of Buddhist art, including incense burners, incense boxes, and water urns made of bronze.

The Joseon era, however, brought a growing trend of suppressing Buddhism in favor of Confucianism. This meant that the bronze objects disappeared, replaced by a wide variety of iron-cast pieces used in the palace and noble homes for both daily and ceremonial life. *Ipsajang* survived the shift from bronze to iron, finding itself adapted to the change of techniques—

namely, the emergence of chiseling. For this process, a chisel was used to flatten out the entire surface of the object, with the silver thread patterns then placed over top.

Apart from being decorated with the silver inlay itself, the surface of the object was often tinted with dark colors using traditional techniques; sometimes, the color and texture of the metal itself was highlighted. The traditional tinting process of darkening the base was intended to create a black-white contrast that would bring out the beauty of the silver. One common method used a mixture of pine soot and vegetable oil. These days, the pine soot is typically replaced by graphite powder. After tinting, the surface is prepared with vegetable oil and finished with a final polishing.

JADE CARVING

While gold has traditionally been prized in both East and West, jade is said to be the "eastern jewel," one held in high regard uniquely by those who are raised in Asian culture. Capturing the gaze with bright, transparent hues, jade is a stone one truly never tires of admiring. In Eastern countries, it was seen as echoing the Confucian scholar and his emphasis on inner maturity—its virtue was harbored deep within.

Korea has a very long history

Kettle made of white jade (by Jang Ju-won)

of jade carving. One site found in the Namgang River basin in Gyeongju dates all the way back to the Neolithic Era. Rings, trinkets, and buttons of jade were key accessories for the upper class from the Three Kingdoms period all the way through to the end of the Joseon era. If the brilliant diamond is the jewel of the sun, then jade, with the gentle beauty it emanates, is like the moonlight.

Once jade is mined, it cannot be exposed to sunlight right away. Having rested deep underground for hundreds of millions of years, it is like the eyes of a person who has lived in a darkened cave and needs time to adjust to the light. In jade's case, it needs time to "catch its breath" in the air. To avoid cracking, it must be wrapped in a moistened straw bag and heated to a very specific temperature (800–1,000°C). The resulting raw jade has a unique grain, and stones from different regions come in different colors, ranging from green to white, yellow, and light brown.

Trimming and pattern engraving is performed with a silk jigsaw. Sand applied at an eight- to nine-degree angle to the thin silk thread is used to grind the stone. Holes are pierced by attaching a point to a bowstring and rubbing the string by hand. Once finished, the jade is polished with powdered rust from nickel silver or iron.

Sedge Weaving

Sedges, known as *wanggol* or *wancho* in Korean, are a type of grass that grows to 1.2–1.5 meters in height and can be found in the rice paddies or wetlands of tropical and temperate regions like Korea and Japan. Readily available to Koreans since time immemorial, sedges have been woven into mats, cushions, plates, sewing baskets, and various other decorations.

Historically, records of sedge use dating back to the Silla era can

Baskets made of flat sedge

be found in the *History of the Three Kingdoms*. During the Goryeo era, kings would perform rituals to the gods of the earth and grain for their people, and sedges were not only laid out below the shrines for the gods' tablets, but also used for various items of bedding in the royal household. Records for the reign of King Taejong (r. 1367–1422) in the *Annals of the Joseon Dynasty* mention sedge items among the gifts sent by the Joseon monarch to the Chinese emperor's household. Woven goods were also reportedly used in the royal household and by the upper class under a variety of names— evidence of the strong reputation they enjoyed.

In more common households, perhaps the most typical sedge items of all are *kkotbangseok* (embroidered flower cushions) and *kkotsamhap* (three-basket sets with flower designs), both of which are carried out using a weft-weaving style. The weaving of sedge requires a sense of precision, weight, and balance born of long

The process of making *hwamunseok* (patterned) mats

experience. It also takes a long time to do the knitwork that makes the weaving beautiful. Many different designs are used, including Chinese characters signifying fortune or abundance, such as 喜 (*hui*, joy) and 福 (*bok*, blessings). Other examples include Arirang patterns and turtles.

To weave an item from sedge, high-quality material is imperative. Sedge is sown in April and moved to a paddy in early May, as with rice. When cultivated in this way, it is ready for harvest in July and August, at which point the stalks are cut and the strips left to dry. Once they take on a blue color, they are soaked in water. After five to six more sessions of sun drying, the strips turn white, meaning that the sedge is now ready for weaving. This is also the time to apply dye for those seeking beautiful coloring in the final material.

Aside from being locally sourced and relatively inexpensive, items made from sedge are well ventilated in summer and effective at absorbing moisture, making them quite practical for storing objects and food. Sedge has also been used in many ways during the winter, thanks to its effective insulation properties.

BAMBOO SCREENS

Bal is a term referring to a traditional screen made of finely cut strips of split reed or bamboo that are tied together with a thin thread. These devices were used to allow for a breeze to pass through a room while shielding doors and windows against sunlight, especially during hot summers. In the olden days, womenfolk were known to utilize these screens to see the bright outside world from within the house, as they had to otherwise stay primarily indoors.

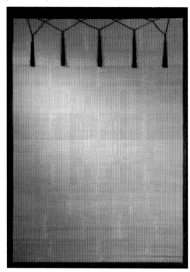

Bamboo *bal* (by Cho Dae-yong)

The ubiquitous *bal* left its traces in all strata of Korean society, from ruler of the country to commoner. This traditional screen went beyond being a simple household essential. It held various roles in the upper levels of society, from being used to shield female royalty when being greeted by her subjects, to shielding the king or prominent ladies when they were out in public, to being part of the wedding palanquin to hide the bride from prying eyes, as well as to partition gazeboes where scholars sought rest.

The reputation of bamboo screens from Tongyeong in Gyeongsangnam-do started when a Joseon Dynasty central military base known as the Navy Headquarters of Tri-Provinces (1603–1895) was established in the region, meant to cater to the three provinces of Chungcheong-do, Jeolla-do, and Gyeongsang-do. Due to the varied supply of diverse materials available at this outpost, Tongyeong saw a boom in the local handicraft industry. It was more than just *bal* that flourished, however; other representative crafts such as *gat* (traditional Korean hats) and lacquerware took off as well.

The process of making a Korean bamboo blind

Compared to the bamboo screens in Japanese and Chinese cultures, Korean bamboo screens evoke a sense of calm and subdued atmosphere. Bamboo is split into slender strips and the delicate weave of the *bal*'s patterned design is its definitive characteristic. Japanese bamboo screens lack this pattern and are often thicker and stiffer, while Chinese bamboo screens, though also finely thin, have their designs painted on at the end, and not woven in during the process.

Windows & Doors

A House of Many Faces

The Korean *hanok* house has many faces. In structural terms, it is hard to draw any hard and fast distinctions between windows (for

The distinction between window and door is less important in a Korean *hanok*, hence they are jointly referred to as *changho* (windows and door).

light and ventilation) and doors (for entering and exiting). Typically, the forms are identical, except the window (*chang*) has a sill, while the door (*mun*) doesn't. As a result, the two are often referred to together as *changho*, each boasting its own beautiful patterns that give the house unique architectural character. Indeed, the number of distinct designs of *hanok* windows and doors is somewhere in the hundreds.

Windows and doors are designed to suit the body frame of the average Korean; sizes are decided by height and shoulder width. The low windows for the "seat of honor"—a seat occupied by seniors in the family—in the *anbang* are positioned at just the right height for someone to rest her elbows on the sill. The sill is set high enough so that someone lying down is not visible from the courtyard. Typically used as barriers to divide different types of space, windows and doors can removed from their frames and be hung on hooks during the summer or at family events, turning the entire interior into a single, open space.

Decorative and Functional

A number of factors must be taken into account when making windows or doors: the amount of light, the strength of the wind, the size of the home, and the preferences of its occupants. A southern-facing window that receives a lot of light requires a long frame pattern to deflect the incoming rays; a house surrounded by trees needs a short frame pattern that allows the light easy access.

Exquisite Crafting

The *hanok* home brings together many different types of wood. No nails are used; instead, timbers are brought together and fitted vertically, horizontally, or diagonally to produce an interlocking shape. *Ieum* joints are formed by fitting wooden parts in the same direction, while *matchum* joints are placed at perpendicular or oblique angles. Together, they offer a scientific technique for generating a unified space with a minimum of timber. Techniques

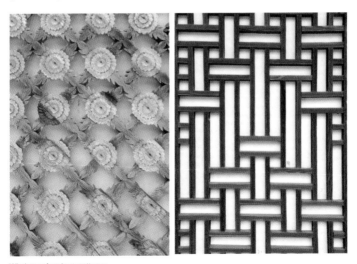

Windows of various patterns

number in the dozens; the most basic *matchum* style, the dovetail joint, is an exquisitely precise method in which pillars, cross-beams, and beams are skillfully brought together to create a framework without nails. The result is a structure that would remain in place even if all the walls were removed and only pillars were left. This same science is also carried over to the making of windows and doors. But rather than being a simple, two-dimensional process of attaching pieces of wood or digging up stumps, it is an architectural process of careful vertical, horizontal, and diagonal connections at the most precisely calibrated proportions.

ROOF TILES

Traditional Korean architecture embodies the people's view of the universe and their sense of aesthetics. Fundamental concepts of Korean cosmology, including principles of *taegeuk* (great absolute), yin and yang, the five elements, circular heaven and square Earth, and the three essential elements, are reflected in Korean construction, while the use of natural materials, such as wood, earth, straw, and paper, represents an effort to realize harmony with nature.

The roof of *hanok*, or a traditional Korean house, is either made with thatch materials or tiles. The line of a thatched roof can be likened to the ridge of a docile cow's back, while that of a tiled roof reminds one of mountain slopes gracing the landscape behind a house, mimicking the agility and gracefulness of a crane's wings just before the bird lands. The elegant lines of either type of traditional roof, with gable or hip-and-gable styles, impart a sense of quiet stability.

The roof is an especially significant component in completing the graceful beauty of Korea's traditional architecture. According to

ancient philosophy, the three essential elements (*samjae*) of the universe are heaven, Earth, and humanity. In traditional architecture, the roof symbolizes heaven and the building's foundation represents Earth. As such, the space between heaven and Earth is the abode of human beings. Given that the *hanok* roof links the space for humans with the heaven above, it stands that it should be the most beautiful aspect of the structure. Therefore, it can be said that the beauty of the roof depends on the capability of the artisan who installs the roof tiles.

Reviving Functional Gracefulness

Even though the earliest usage of roof tiles in Korea is still unknown, excavated sites support the popularity of roof tiling since the Three Kingdoms period. Roof tiles are made from clay that has been shaped into a curved form. Being fired at extremely high

Roof and roof-end tiles of a traditional Korean *hanok* roof

temperatures of 1,000–2,000°C, they are exceptionally durable, but only those without any cracks or deformities are used to build roofs.

In accordance with yin and yang principles, there are two types of tiles: male (convex) and female (concave). This holds for the roof-end tiles as well. The female tiles are laid following the tiles' natural curvature, starting from the center of the roof, down to the eaves. Three overlapping tiles form a unit to ensure that the roof would not leak even if two of the tiles were to crack. A mortar made of mud is plastered in between female tiles for the male tiles to affix, and these tiles are laid in straight lines from the end of the rafters to the top of the roof ridge. Earthen mortar is used to prevent the tiles from slipping out of position.

ONGGI WARE

In addition to creating bacteria that are beneficial to the human body, the process of fermentation also produces a rich, ripe flavor that many find has an oddly attractive quality. In fact, futurist Alvin Toffler predicted in *The Third Wave* (1980) that fermented foods would eventually be seen as the taste of the future. He foresaw the world's food culture turning its attention away from the current preference for salt and prepared sauces and more toward fermented foods. Fermentation enhances the nutritional value of foods by producing a variety of beneficial by-products. About 90 percent of Korean food involves fermentation, and *onggi* (pottery vessels) have been thought of as the ideal containers for Korean food to assist in the fermentation process.

Onggi ware is used to ferment food.

Breathing Pots

Making a traditional *onggi* vessel involves a laborious process of kneading cold, tough clay; shaping it as it circles on a spinning wheel; and, finally, firing it in a kiln stoked with oak wood. While Korean *onggi* can come in *oji geureut* (glazed) style or *jil geureut* (unglazed) style, the term *onggi* has come to reference *oji geureut* as unglazed varieties are rarely seen anymore. *Onggi* are also referred to as "breathing jars" because micro-fine pores on *onggi* surfaces allow for air circulation to facilitate fermentation, yet are also able to restrict the moisture that would cause the jars' contents to spoil. Korean womenfolk take great care to keep *onggi* surfaces clean to allow the pores to breathe properly and help perfect their stored kimchi and soy sauce.

Aging Clay for Its Breathing Function

Onggi clay should be properly aged to assure the vessel's breathing function. The importance of aging is reflected in the following saying among potters: "Clay you're preparing today is best if used by your grandson." There are diverse regional differences in Korean clay in how crumbly, sticky, gritty, or fine the clay may be. Consequently, in order to procure different clay types to have a better mix to work with, potters travel all over the country in search of regions famous for their soil conditions to collect samples and to discover the best possible combinations through trial and error.

Once this desirable clay ratio is obtained, the combined mixture is submerged in water to filter out impurities, such as grass roots and grit, before it is aged. Following this, the clay is thoroughly dried and pounded to be mixed with water and then kneaded well to rid it of air. The final product is a sticky mixture that can be shaped into coils resembling long strands of Korean rice cake.

These pieces are then placed on a white clay powder–dusted pottery wheel and spread and pounded into the desired shape for

The process of making *onggi*

the *onggi*'s base. Coils of clay are piled in layers along the base's edge and pulled up to form the vessel's walls. By layering the strands, the walls become thin yet also sturdy. Once a potter has finished molding the clay, it is left to dry for a period of one to four weeks, depending on the season. After the *onggi* is thoroughly dried, it is coated with a glaze of wood ash and red clay mixed and left to age for two to four months. It typically takes 50 to 60 days to complete the entire process, from the preparation of clay to the firing of the final pieces.

Onggi is generally produced four times a year—twice in spring and twice in the fall. Each kiln, stocked with thin-barked oak wood, can churn out 350–400 pieces. The temperature in the kilns rises from 100°C on the first day up to 1,200–1,300°C by the fifth day, after which point the fire is extinguished.

BELL CASTING

Buddhist culture developed early on in Korean history, and the *beomjong* bell was one of the ceremonial items crafted for the deliverance of human beings. Temple bells were first used in ancient India to help citizens tell time. As the Buddha's message of truth and mercy spread through the world, they became a means of enlightening people and delivering them to the world of the Buddha.

The countries of the Eastern Buddhist sphere, including China, Korea, Japan, and the nations of Southeast Asia, typically had their own characteristic temple bells; the appearance of an "Eastern bell" could vary greatly from one setting to the next. In simple terms, Korean bells are shaped like overturned kimchi urns, Chinese bells resemble upside-down tulips, and Japanese bells look like inverted drinking glasses.

The biggest difference between Eastern and Western bells is the manner in which they are struck. With Western bells, a clapper is hung inside the structure, and the bell itself is shaken to produce sound. For Eastern bells, a *dangjwa* ("striking seat") is made on the bell's surface and struck with a *dangmok* ("striking wood").

Even among Eastern bells, Korean bells are renowned for their quality. They are admired for the elegant and beautiful designs engraved into the bell's surface, but most of the praise focuses on the sound: clear, with a soft and long-lasting resonance. While Chinese bells are made of iron, Korean temple bells are all cast from bronze, a material that may account for their ability to move listeners with a broader, fuller sound than the iron produces.

Temple bells are the largest of Korea's metal crafts. Their greatest development came under Unified Silla, a tradition that carried over into Goryeo. Bell production grew scarcer under the Joseon Dynasty, which revered Confucian values and worked to suppress Buddhism. By the late Joseon period, the difficult traditional casting

海印梵鐘

Buddhist bell in Haeinsa Temple, Hapcheon,
Gyeongsangnam-do

styles had been abandoned in favor of the simpler Chinese method of temple bell making. The long tradition, dating back all the way to Unified Silla, was in danger of dying completely.

It was in the late 1990s, however, that the traditional method started making a comeback, thanks to the efforts of a man named Won Kwang-sik, a master craftsman who started making bells in the early 1960s. Distressed by the lack of information existing on traditional bell construction in Korea, he decided to seek out specialists in the field and form a research association with a handful of like-minded individuals. They were soon joined by art historians, general historians, and acoustic specialists. Their efforts finally paid off in 1997 with the restoration of the traditional lost-wax casting method of bell production.

Lost-wax casting, or the creation of metal works using a series of rubber and wax molds, had been used throughout the Unified Silla, Goryeo, and Joseon periods to produce Korea's greatest bells, designated National Treasures like the Sacred Bell of Great King

Goryeo Dynasty copper bell

Seongdeok and the Bronze Bell of Sangwonsa Temple. The process of lost-wax casting is complex, demands advanced technology, and takes a very long time. As a result, the odds of failure are high. If successful, however, the resulting pattern, surface, and sound are more exquisite than anything produced by other methods.

The Sacred Bell of Great King Seongdeok, also known as the "Emille Bell," is considered the greatest example of a bell made through lost-wax casting. It is renowned for its spellbinding sound quality. Professor Lee Jang-mu of Seoul National University spent over three years analyzing its undulations (the particular wave pattern produced from striking a hollow surface like a glass or

Won Kwang-sik, temple bell iron caster

bell, with sounds weakening and strengthening like a pulse) and the different vibrations on the bell surface that produced them. He concluded that the unique, lasting *ah-ang, ah-ang* sound pattern when the bell is struck is formed by countless individual sounds within the harmony of individual sounds that cancel each other over time. Lee found no fewer than 50 different frequencies within the 1,000 Hz (1,000 cycles per second) range alone. In contrast, the Great Paul bell at Britain's St. Paul's Cathedral, cast in 1881, produces less than 20.

An estimated 300 temple bells survive in Korea today. Around 50 of them are classified as National Treasures or Treasures. Visitors can see restored versions of the bells at the Jincheon Bell Museum, founded in Jincheon, Chungcheongbuk-do, in 2005.

4

MASTERS OF CRAFT

The Korean term *jangin* is used in many fields to describe people who spend their lives learning and mastering a traditional technique handed down from the past. In English, they might be called "master craftspeople." The *jangin* uses his or her store of technique, forged by years of experience and practice, to infuse personal intent into ordinary items for daily use. Their crafts are products of exceptional skill and understanding in a particular field, and it is thanks to their efforts that Korea can boast of the exceptional craft culture it does.

Historically, however, the social status of the *jangin* was quite low. *Jangin* were especially despised during the Joseon era, when Confucianism dominated thought. The national economy depended on agriculture, and the rulers emphasized farming while discouraging commerce. The most revered class in a Confucian society was that of the *seonbi*, the aristocratic scholar; after that came the farmers. Farmers produced the crops that were so vital to economic production, but they were also politically important, accounting as they did for the bulk of the population. The *jangin*, artisans who produced items for daily living, were viewed as having the same status as the merchants who profited from selling goods: a "surplus class."

The only situations where *jangin* were truly valued was when they produced the items needed for state projects, or the daily essentials required by the ruling *yangban* class. Under the strict caste system of Joseon Korea, most *jangin* came from the ranks of government slaves or civilians. They were enlisted to provide the government with their handiwork for a certain length of time, after which they returned to running their own craft industry. Naturally, such specialists were also required to pay a "craft tax" to the state.

Fan maker, the late Lee Ki-dong

Government slaves who were seen as having particular technical skill might have the opportunity to advance through official government servitude to become artisans.

Because the social climate was so rigorous about status and hostile to commerce, *jangin* were long denied treatment commensurate with their skill and labor. The opening of Korea with the Japan-Korea Treaty of 1876 only meant a greater ordeal. Also known as the Japan-Korea Treaty of Amity, this trade agreement was Joseon's first treaty based in modern international law, but its terms were highly unequal, imposed by Japan more or less at gunpoint.

Besides its political importance, the opening of Korea also brought major structural change to the popular economy. Western-style modernization meant a capitalist economy, and this in turn depended upon factory-style, mechanized industries that would allow mass-production. Joseon was soon taken over by cheap, mass-produced products from the West; under the Japanese occupation, colonial policy would hasten the development of mechanized industry. It was in this historical climate that Koreans became used to products that were mass-produced, standardized, and inexpensive. The techniques and labor of the *jangin* barely hung on, preserved in the hands of a smattering of practitioners.

Drum maker, the late Park Sam-hong

Korean master crafters (clockwise) Kwon Yeong-hak (bow making), Kim Geuk-cheon (metal ornaments), Han Sang-soo (embroidery), the late Lee In-se (tray-tables)

In the wake of liberation from Japanese rule and the ensuing Korean War, the country was in utter ruin socially, economically, and culturally. Entire traditions had been uprooted, and philosophical confusion deepened. It was at this point that a wave of Western culture, chiefly from the United States, began hitting Korean shores. Westernized industry first began in the mid-1950s, but the country had yet to reach contemporary levels of development. Craft practitioners, for their part, were given little opportunity to shine.

Korean master crafters (left to right) Kim Ki-chan (pyrograph), Lee Hyung-man (lacquer painting), Jang Ju-won (jade craft), Kim Hee-jin (knotwork)

Things began to change with the creation of a craft division at the National Art Exhibition, a state effort launched in the 1950s. Suddenly, craftspeople were enjoying a status comparable to that of artists. The 1960s were a time of diverse ideas, and crafts began gaining recognition as a field of valuable creative work. By the start of the decade, more and more people were acknowledging craftspeople, their creative activities, and the items they created as a respectable occupation in the contemporary cultural context. Another change occurred with the passing of the 1962 Cultural Heritage Promotion Act: As it were, *jangin* who had mastered traditional handicraft techniques were now eligible for selection as Important Intangible Cultural Heritage—a signal of the growing social recognition they were coming to enjoy.

THE ARTISANS OF JOSEON

Crafts under the Joseon Dynasty were a highly specialized field. In general, they were classified into two types: general handicrafts and palace crafts. These categories can be broken down in turn into government, workshop, temple, peasant, and *baekjeong* (butcher's class) varieties. The practices of the workshop, temple, and *baekjeong* craftspeople were full-time jobs, while peasant crafts were typically seen as more of a hobby.

The *Gyeongguk daejeon* (National Code of Law) lists two categories of *jangin*: the artisans of the capital and those practicing outside. Capital artisans were registered in Hanseongbu (today's Seoul), while outside artists were registered external to the capital region in the part of the country known as *jibang*, or "regions outside of Hanseong." A total of 2,795 types of capital artisans in 129 areas were prescribed in the *Gyeongguk daejeon*; for outside artisans, the categories numbered 3,764 in 27 areas. The 129 areas in the first category include many that are familiar to people today, with specialties in forging, lacquer, woodwork, porcelain, urns, leather, bookmaking, paintings, and paper.

Mat Weaving
by Kim Hong-do
(18th Century)

Chapter Five

CRAFTS AND PATTERNS

Patterns are a crucial part of any discussion on crafts. Schematic representations of points, lines, and color created for an aesthetic response, the cultural significance of patterns extends beyond craftwork and into the spatial composition of painting and architecture. Their beauty enables them to have a decorative function, but they are also symbolic expressions of inherent human wishes and desires.

A pattern is akin to a symbol, with an agreed-upon meaning among the groups that appreciate it. Simply viewing the pattern is enough to make people respond to the intentions and values it represents. It has an almost incantatory logic: As we recall the values represented by an item, it becomes imbued with a sense of practical desire and comes to express the hope that those values can become a reality.

Many of the patterns used in Korea's traditional crafts are expressions of worldly values, the shared wishes of the population: abundant blessings, riches, long life and fecundity, or simple virtues. A peony in full blossom represents a wish for wealth. The pomegranate or grape designs that decorate a woman's space echo the incantatory desire for an abundance of sons.

In short, traditional patterns are powerfully charged expressions of the practical desire for a perfect life. They come in many varieties, which can be classified by their subject matter and meaning.

PEOPLE

One category of pattern involves representation of human faces and forms, as well as mystical hermits, Buddhas, the four heavenly guardians of Buddhism, and goblins. Historically, Buddhism was a

Dancheong refers to a traditional style of multicolor decorative painting on wooden buildings, strictly in accordance with the five elements governing the order of the universe

Patterns of goblins were carved onto roofs, bridges, windows, and doors as symbols of protection against evil.

very important religion in Korea, and images of the Buddha, the Four Devas, and flying maidens are frequent motifs. One of the most common patterns for daily life involves the *dokkaebi*, or goblin.

The origins of the *dokkaebi* motif can be traced to China's *taotie* (饕餮) pattern. The *taotie* was another mythical creature, with large eyes and a gaping mouth with protruding canines. Its eyesight was said to be so powerful that it could locate any evil demons that were lurking nearby. But while the *taotie* patterns of China were quite threatening and bold in their imagery, Korea's *dokkaebi* images have a much more human, comical aspect.

Dokkaebi patterns were often engraved on rooftops, bridges, windows, and doors to serve as guardians driving away evil.

ANIMALS

Animals are both things of benefit and objects of fear to humans, and they have often been a motif for pattern designs. These representations capture not just the animal's form, but also its symbolism within the human unconscious. Some of the animals are actual creatures, such as fish, but others are imaginary beasts like dragons and *haechi* (unicorn-lions). For daily items, the butterfly may be the most beloved of animal designs. Symbolizing natural love, beauty, and marital bliss, it was used in a broad range of women's accessories and furniture.

The Dragon

As king of the animals, the dragon was seen as a creature of unlimited power, possessing skills and strength that humans could scarcely fathom. It also appears as the presiding beast for all natural phenomena. Sometimes it was shown ruling floods and droughts;

The mythical *haechi* (left) and dragon

Left: Phoenix patterns on the attire of Joseon Dynasty queens
Right: Fish symbolizing leisure and pleasure, as well as the prosperity of one's descendants

other times, it was an ocean god that governed seafaring and shipping. Its power was its ability to ward off evil and bring blessings. In Buddhist art, the dragon was one of eight guardian spirits protecting the buddhadharma and could often been seen decorating the tops of temple bells. In the palace, the dragon pattern symbolized the majesty of the monarch. Engraved on tiles, the dragon design was used to prevent evil from entering the structure or the household. Dragon designs were also carved into knife handles or placed at the opening of tea kettles to keep evil energy from getting inside.

The Phoenix

The Korean word for phoenix is *bonghwang*, which encompasses both male (*bong*) and female (*hwang*) sexes. This mythical bird is said to have been born of a love affair between the dragon (the king of animals) and a crane. Likened to a king or queen for its noble and dignified stature, it was an auspicious animal that heralded peace and prosperity and was often used as a palace pattern. Perhaps the best example of a phoenix design is one found on a gold-copper incense burner dating back to the Baekje era. A phoenix was also inscribed on the head of the *jam*, a decorative hairpin worn by the queen, and beautiful phoenix patterns can be found embroidered on her other garments as well.

Fish

Fish patterns symbolized a variety of things: leisure, enjoyment, worldly success, filial piety, prosperous grandchildren, and marital bliss. Chuang-tzu, considered one of the foremost philosophers of Daoism, invented the term *yule* (魚樂), or "the happiness of the fish," as he looked down on the animal's peaceful underwater frolicking. The animals eventually came to represent ease and pleasure in life.

PLANTS

Plants have often been used in patterns for their beauty and utility in human life. Flowers are a particularly common theme; even when it carries no particular symbolic meaning, the flower has stood as a representation of beauty itself.

Some of the most frequent plant designs are the lotus and the vine. Known for its hardiness and vigor, the lotus has long been appreciated far and wide as a design for living. Examples of these

Due to their beauty, flowers are a usual theme for patterns.

patterns can be found on tiles from the Three Kingdoms era, Goryeo celadon, and various implements from the Joseon period. It came to represent cleanliness and purity because of its natural setting: growing in the mud of the wetlands, yet remaining untainted by it.

Vines have the meaning of continuation, and the hope for long life and good things that last. Vine patterns were also frequently used as a way of highlighting other designs.

ARTIFICAL PATTERNS

Some of the designs in Korean crafts used human-made patterns that resemble neither fauna nor flora. These tended to be objects that symbolized human benefit or good omens. One of the best examples is the *chilbo* pattern. The name means "seven jewels," referring to coins, water buffalo horns, picture books, wormwood, and mirrors. It also refers to two themes specifically drawn out of Korean traditional culture: the *bangseung* and *teukgyeong*.

Among these symbols incorporated into patterns, the coin and buffalo horn symbolize blessings, while the picture book, a schematic representation of a drawing pad and book, signified happiness and wealth—the easy life of the government official. Wormwood leaves, often used in Chinese medicine, also served to help start fires. This only added to their value, and they came to represent long life and luck. Mirrors represented fecundity and were seen as emblems of the king and the ruling class. At the time when these other symbols were being incorporated into pattern imagery,

A copper coin pattern, one of the seven treasures, decorates the outside of a ceramic vessel.

the *bangseung*—a triangular gold paper ornament that was hung on the corners or ends of the cloth packages (*bojagi*) used on special occasions—expressed a wish for good things to happen. The *teukgyeong*, by contrast, was an ancient musical instrument made with jade or stone. Similar in shape to the Chinese character for person (人), it was prized for its sound.

NATURAL SCENERY

Patterns based on natural scenery often depicted the sun, the moon, clouds, and stars. They typically symbolized long life; as heavenly bodies, they far outlived human beings. Cloud patterns were a particularly common natural motif. Clouds are ever-changing as they drift through the sky, possessing both inner force and a mixture of strength and weakness, hollowness and substance. Koreans of old

believed that a person who amassed enough virtue in this life would ascend to the heavens or achieve buddhahood atop a cloud. Clouds were also one of the ten symbols of longevity. In many cases, clouds were used like vines to highlight other patterns. Other examples include *sansu* motifs, which recall landscape paintings, and *goeseok* motifs, which depict oddly shaped rocks.

Letters and Characters

For some patterns, letters or characters are used as a sign, with patterns formed through the positioning of the same character in a row. Letters that are seen as having positive meanings are inscribed on objects to express the wish that their meaning will come to pass. The two most notable examples are the characters *su* (壽), meaning "long life," and *bok* (福), meaning "blessings" or "fortune." Back before medical science had truly developed, long life was the greatest blessing of all. This may explain why so many of the patterns created by the Koreans of old are symbolic of longevity. Sometimes turtles or peaches were shown as common representations of long life, but other times the *su* character itself was used to wish for longevity. Character patterns were especially

Geometric patterns for window grates

common as embroidery on clothing, or as wood rice cake and confectionary molds. It was a way of placing the hope for a healthy family on even the most everyday of items.

GEOMETRIC PATTERNS

The category of *gihamun*, or geometric patterns, includes designs that show circles and horizontal, vertical, and diagonal lines. *Gihamun* patterns are essentially just lines and figures, but they are especially significant because they are one of the most primeval of designs—the very first attempted by humankind when it started creating patterns in the prehistoric era. Tools created during the Neolithic Era and Bronze Age show series of line, circle, and concentric circle patterns, which are said to have been these

Wall decorated with various geometric patterns

societies' way of representing the sun, its rays, and the rain.

MIXED PATTERNS

Not all patterns involve choosing just one motif. Mixed patterns are, as their name suggests, mixtures of different themes. A dragon, symbolizing the driving away of evil, might be paired with a cloud to highlight its auspicious nature. Other common examples included the apricot, symbolizing spring and longevity, and a bird called the *palgajo* (literally the "bird of eight songs"), which represented devotion to one's parents. It eventually became common to pair patterns of similar meanings, or to create a new symbol by combining different meanings.

Chapter Six

KOREAN CRAFTS TODAY AND TOMORROW

Korea's crafts and their rich history are drawing renewed attention today. In the 1960s, a campaign was launched to rediscover and recreate the values of traditional crafts. The list of human cultural heritage that is being passed on to a new generation has grown to include Silla earthenware, metal crafts, stone crafts, Goryeo celadon and mother-of-pearl lacquerware, and Joseon-era *buncheong* ware, white porcelain, woodwork, horn crafts, masks, and metalcraft.

Many other efforts have focused on putting a modern spin on traditional crafts and bringing them into the design industry. There are a number of reasons for this: frustration with mass-production, uniformity, rationality, and monotony wrought by industrialization and mechanized culture, as well as a newfound awareness of lifestyle aesthetics and traditional artistry. More and more designers are applying traditional craft techniques to modern product design and production methods, demonstrating the contemporary applications and appeal of these approaches. Their work has brought a new awareness of traditional crafts, and the reception from Korean and international audiences alike has been quite favorable.

Meanwhile, the introduction of crafts to university education and art competitions has helped raise its status to that of fine art. The 1970s were a period of rapid development in modern industry, which naturally spawned fields of industrial design and modern crafts. These areas attracted an increasing number of students to the applied arts and craft departments of Korea's universities. In

Visitors to a Korean handicraft trade fair

spite of the positive aspects of this development, this trend was overwhelmingly focused on the art aspect of the crafts. Today, there is a growing movement away from that emphasis, and instead toward a return to the essential role of crafts in Korean society. "Crafts as part of life" has been the slogan, with more and more examples of "lifestyle crafts" produced by small-scale studios. At the same time, a growing variety of craft fairs and craft schools have contributed to developing a base for the industry.

Left: Visitors looking at work at a Korean handicraft fair in London
Right: Visitors at Milano Design Week viewing Korean traditional crafts that have been given a new twist

A FRESH TAKE ON TRADITION

One designer who has been especially busy translating a reinterpretation of traditional crafts into a modern style of design is Been Kim. Previously an industrial designer for cell phones, Kim has dedicated herself to finding a design style that is uniquely Korean.

Famous examples include her *hanji* (Korean paper) basket, an application of her research into the properties of this traditional craft and its techniques, or her brocade patterned block mats, which use the tones and forms of traditional *dancheong* paintwork. Both have been praised for their new spin on the beauty of traditional patterns. Other items include pouches, wallets, and storage containers made with the laminated paper used for flooring in traditional homes. Kim's brand, called Meeets, offers a wide range

1

2

3

Been Kim's Traditional Craft-Influenced Designs

1. *Made of Chair*: This easy chair is made with straw from Dangjin, a city in Korea's Chungcheongnam-do. Kim sought to convey the image of one of Korea's wintry mountains with the simple, comfortable feel of straw and its crisp sensations and smell. The bottom is wrapped to provide stable support; farther up, the natural spreading of the rice sheaf ends offers gentle support for the back.

2. Dancheong Ornament Series: Items include *hanji* (Korean paper) thank-you cards and accessories using the *dancheong* grass designs of Gyeongbokgung Palace as a pattern motif.

3. *Hanji* Baskets: Handmade items applying traditional Korean papermaking techniques, these baskets are dyed with a variety of natural ingredients from all over Korea, including volcanic ash from Jejudo Island, mud from the West Sea coastal flats, oak soot, and India ink.

of items that interpret traditional Korean crafts like *maedeup* knots and *dancheong*-style images in a way that meets the needs of modern living.

Mother-of-pearl lacquerware is a craft with a millennia-old history in Korea, and its items are among the most frequently given craft gifts presented to foreign heads of state when they visit. One studio is now working to blend the craft's techniques with modern colors and forms to create a new brand of furniture and daily essentials. Established in 1978, the CheongBong Lacquer Studio brings together a group of traditional artisans and designers to produce furniture, containers, gifts, and essentials using lacquer, mother-of-pearl, pure gold, and other natural materials. Its goal is to "make crafts a part of life," with everything from high-quality small-batch productions to accessories for a wide customer base. Attention is given to form, material, size, production method, and packaging. The studio's airtight earthenware with hardwood varnish has been singled out for praise as a combination of lacquer crafts with classic pottery styles to aid fermentation and natural maturation. Admirers have called it a nature-friendly option free from environmental hormones, with a convenient shape for stacking in the refrigerator.

UNESCO PICKS TOP KOREAN HANDICRAFTS

In 2008, an international judging committee met in Beijing to bestow UNESCO certification on outstanding examples of East Asia handicrafts. Among the 56 works submitted by Korea—textiles, pottery, woodwork, and various other craft areas—11 of Korea's traditional crafts were among those selected. The UNESCO Award of Excellence for Handicrafts system was established to certify quality and open up sales markets for crafts by protecting dying traditional arts and supporting the creation of new craft items for modern life.

1. Bowl with *buncheong* "burst" pattern, Danwon Doye (Cho Min-ho)
2. Danyang white porcelain brass rice bowl set, Korean Craft Museum, Cheongju (Seo Young-gi)
3. Traditional white porcelain dolls, Leejabang (Lee Hong-ja)
4. Stew pots, Sonnae Onggi (Lee Hyun-bae)
5. Bamboo bowl set, Jigang Doyo (Kim Pan-ki)
6. *Cheomjang* tea set, Y.C Ceramic Studio (Yun Ju-cheol)
7. White porcelain cloud tea kettle, Ceramic Studio 2trees (Lee Kyoung-han)
8. Moon jar, Sonnae Onggi (Lee Hyun-bae)
9. Gium I, Gallery [O:N] (Lee Eun-hee)
10. Embroidered business card case, Korea Imperial Embroidery Research Institute (Kim Tae-ja)
11. Korean Feeling, Beadsborn Academy (Lee Jong-rye)

APPENDIX

INFORMATION

CRAFT-RELATED ORGANIZATIONS

Korea Craft & Design Foundation (KCDF)

A public institution of the Ministry of Culture, Sports and Tourism, KCDF carries out businesses related to the promotion and proliferation of Korean handicraft and design culture. This includes research, publication, education, exhibition, and domestic/overseas collaborative efforts to pursue projects to develop design culture.

- Website: https://www.kcdf.kr/kcdf/main/userMain/main.do

Office
- Address: 53 Haeyoung Yulgokro Hall 5th Floor, Jongno-gu, Seoul
- Tel: 82-2-398-7900

KCDF Gallery Shop

A space for leading Korean craft artisans and designers to display and sell handmade crafts

- Address: 11-gil, Insa-dong, Jongno-gu, Seoul
- Tel: 82-2-732-9382

Korean Crafts Council

Founded in 1973, the Korean Crafts Council (KCC) promotes the creative activities of Korean craftspeople, publishes and promotes handicraft-related material, and promotes international exchanges pertaining to Korean handicraft. A yearly members' exhibition has been held since 1974.

• Website: http://craftkorea.org/
• Tel: 82-2-324-4529

CRAFT-RELATED EVENTS

Handarty Korea

A unique domestic handicraft and cultural festival operating since 2011 that allows visitors to see and experience a diverse range of handmade, handcrafted artwork

• Website: www.handarty.co.kr

Korea Crafts Culture Expo

A yearly craft exhibition held every fall that features traditional handicrafts, lifestyle projects, interior design pieces, traditional musical instruments, and souvenirs. Experiential programs allow visitors a chance to try making pottery and hanji.

• Website: www.kocce.or.kr

Cheongju Craft Biennale

Held every other year since 1999, the Cheongju Craft Biennale provides an opportunity to revitalize interest in the value of crafts. A comprehensive collection of crafts and design trends, from metalwork, ceramics, and glass to textiles and wood painting, has been featured over the last seven events, with the hope of opening up new horizons in the world of crafts.

• Website: http://www.okcj.org/

Craft Platform

Established in 2014, this event is meant to foster handicraft industries to meet the growing domestic and international interest in Korean crafts, and also to innovate crafts ranging from items for pure viewing, to functional and useable works.

Home-Table Deco Fair

A home décor fair held yearly in Seoul, Busan, and Daegu since 2005 to exhibit furniture, home styling pieces, light fixtures, and interior pieces

• Website: www.hometabledeco.co.kr/main/main.php

Korea Crafts Competition

The longest-running craft-related event in Korea, run by the Korea Federation of Handicrafts Cooperatives since 1971

• Website: www.crafts.or.kr

The content of this book has been compiled, edited, and supplemented from the articles published in:

KOREANA, VOL. 18, NO. 3, AUTUMN 2004
"Even More Beautiful with the Passage of Time" by Ryu Min

KOREANA, VOL. 18, NO. 4, WINTER 2004
"Silver Inlay Master and Creator of Heartfelt Artwork" by Ryu Min

KOREANA, VOL. 19, NO. 1, SPRING 2005
"Jang Ju-won's Lifelong Passion and Dedication to Jadecraft" by Ryu Min

KOREANA, VOL. 19, NO. 3, AUTUMN 2005
"Maker of Bronze Temple Bells with Sublime Resonance" by Park Ok-soon

KOREANA, VOL. 21, NO. 2, SUMMER 2007
"Master Craftsman of Traditional Bamboo Screens" by Lee Min-young

KOREANA, VOL. 21, NO. 3, AUTUMN 2007
"Exemplifies the Tradition of Soban" by Lee Min-young

KOREANA, VOL. 21, NO. 4, WINTER 2007
"Yi Sang-jae Handicrafter of Sedge Masterpieces" by Lee Min-young

KOREANA, VOL. 22, NO. 1, SPRING 2008
"Each and Every Stitch Must be Perfect" by Lee Min-young

KOREANA, VOL. 23, NO. 2, SUMMER 2009
"Bang Yeon-Ok Weaves Ramie Fabric as Light as Dragonfly Wings" by Park Hyun-sook

KOREANA, VOL. 23, NO. 4, WINTER 2009
"Shoemaker Hwang Hae-bong" by Park Hyun-sook

PHOTOGRAPHS

CREDITS

Publisher	Kim Hyung-geun
Editor	Lee Jin-hyuk
Assistant Editor	Shin Yesol
Copy Editor	Jamie Stief
Translators	Colin A. Mouat, Lim Jiaying
Proofreader	Anna Bloom
Designer	Son Hong-kyeong